BROOKLANDS COLLEGE LIBRARY
HEATH ROAD, WEYBRIDGE, SURREY KT13 8TT
Tel. (0932) 853300 Ext. 344

156496048x

This item should be returned on or before the last date
entered below. If desired, an extension on the loan period
may be granted on application to the Librarian.

DATE OF RETURN	DATE OF RETURN	DATE OF RETURN
-9. SEP. 1996	-7. FEB. 2005	
-4. JUN. 1996	21. FEB. 2006	
29. NOV. 1996	1.7.65	
-2. JUL. 1997	18. JAN. 2007	
25. JAN. 1999	-3. OCT. 2007	
23. MAY. 2001	06 JAN 2009	
15. FEB. 2002	-2 JUN 2009	
-7. OCT. 2002	1.1 JAN 2012	
26. FEB. 2004		
-6. MAY 2004		

AUTHOR ....

TITLE .... GREAT T-SHIRT GRAPHICS

CLASSIFICATION NO. .... 7⧸⧸⧸ 746.6

ACCESSION NO. 061907

061907

Copyright©1993 by Rockport Publishers, Inc.

All rights reserved. No part of this book may be reproduced in any form without written permission of the copyright owners. All images in this book have been reproduced with the knowledge and prior consent of the artists concerned and no responsibility is accepted by producer, publisher or printer for any infringement of copyright or otherwise, arising from the contents of this publication. Every effort has been made to ensure that credits accurately comply with information supplied.

First published in the United States of America by:
Rockport Publishers, Inc.
146 Granite Street
Rockport, Massachusetts 01966
Telephone: (508) 546-9590
Fax: (508) 546-7141
Telex: 5106019284 ROCKORT PUB

Distributed to the book trade and art trade in the U.S. and Canada by:
North Light, an imprint of
F & W Publications
1507 Dana Avenue
Cincinnati, Ohio 45207
Telephone: (513) 531-2222

Other Distribution by:
Rockport Publishers, Inc.
Rockport, Massachusetts 01966

ISBN 1-56496-048-X

10 9 8 7 6 5 4 3 2 1

Designer: Amy Elizabeth Farr
Cover Illustration: David Cowles
Editor: Rosalie Grattaroti
Production Manager: Barbara States

Printed in Singapore by Regent Publishing

GREAT T~SHIRT
graphics

BROOKLANDS COLLEGE LIBRARY
WEYBRIDGE, SURREY KT13 8TT

ROCKPORT
PUBLISHERS

Rockport Publishers ～ Rockport, Massachusetts

PWANNGG!!

It pops into their head like a favorite cartoon sound. "I'm With Stupid" with a finger pointing to the left, ironed on to a white polyester/cotton blend T-shirt. This is what my mom's friends think of when she tells them what her weird son Mike does for a living. Yup! That's me, the "textile screen printer," or in other words, a nice name for "T-shirt printer." It's an occupation of which I've always been embarrassed. Mainly because of the horrendous and idiotic designs that have plagued this industry. • But T-shirt design has come a long way baby. From dime store and comic book novelty, the T-shirt has mutated into advertising billboard, political propaganda, fashion statement and finally, an icon of popular American culture. Yikes! • The printed T-shirt first began proliferating modern American culture in the late 60's, and let's face it, design on T-shirts was lacking (to say the least). Undoubtedly designers of the time looked down on the lowly T-shirt, sneering at the juvenile and many times moronic sayings and images people proudly wore on their chests. The past 20 years has changed this attitude. As the T-shirt became more popular and entrenched itself into our culture, design improved and matured. • Designers of a generation ago never had a chance or even thought to design a T-shirt—mainly because no one ever thought to print on one. But today's designers grew up wearing the T-shirt as fashion, never remembering a time without it and therefore accepting

100% cotton as a semi-legitimate medium for design. It's a good bet every graphic design major today has tried their hand at designing a T-shirt before graduation. • Now, in the 90's, classic works of art from Dali, Van Gogh and Remington have been reproduced as traveling wearable art galleries. Famous artists and graphic designers are contracted to design lines of T-shirts. Ad agencies and design firms are asked to produce T-shirts on a regular basis for their corporate clients. Even today's most heralded and talented designers see the T-shirt as a legitimate challenge to their abilities. • I've spent nights awake wondering why a book like this hasn't been published sooner. I spent equal amounts of time kicking myself for not doing this myself. But now, I realize why this book hasn't been done before. I can't lie and tell you inane, poorly designed T-shirts still don't dominate the market because you know they do. But times have have changed, (especially over the past five years), and only today has the T-shirt gained and deserved respect as a legitimate medium for design and communication. That's why you're reading this book today. • This book showcases some of the best designed T-shirts that today's most talented designers have to offer. I hope these pieces inspire more designers to design for the T-shirt, realizing its full potential and not consider it an ugly stepchild. I'm already trying to convince the publishers to make this an annual project (hint, hint). • But the best thing about this book is now I can stop lying every time I'm asked that perennial favorite cocktail party question "So, what do you do for a living?"

Michael V. Timble, Marketing & Sales Manager, Propaganda Screenprinting/Chicago

Screenprinting garments

There is a particular uniqueness to it -- it's a medium that exists in a precarious gray zone between bumper stickers, black velvet painting, and greeting cards. Almost everyone has at least met someone who has seen a T-shirt. It's success is based on the lack of pretension, because t-shirts are considered a casual garment, and they don't cost any more than that hideous set of salt and pepper shakers shaped like the gates of Graceland. We project a vast array of messages with these mobile billboards, running the gamut from rock propaganda and athletic support, to tourism and art advocacy. The messages become uncommonly personal in their proximity to the wearer's being, as well as their ability to change with one's moods. Because the image on a shirt exists as a 3 dimensional object and exists in a borderless space, it becomes almost iconic. • There are tricks and techniques that make this graphic process a craft in its own right. Unlike offset printing there are very few rules or industry guidelines. Most of these screen artisans started in a garage or basement somewhere and found their own ways to make it work. Struggling with fast-drying waterbased inks and homemade screens and presses, they started with simple emblems and logos. The development of durable plastic-

is a grass roots art form.

based ink formulations saw these underground craftsmen expanding their vocabulary of techniques day by day. Multicolor work began to grow in popularity and the expertise required to print complex images on T-shirts has become a science in its own right. • The personal computer has recently revolutionized the range of possibilities for this once homespun art form. Darkroom moles and rubylith butchers now can visualize and manipulate so much more completely the final product that they are striving for. Once sacred methods such as 4-color process separating and other high-end photographic techniques are becoming commonplace. • As of this writing there are a wealth of applications and supporting platforms that can be used for very sophisticated reproduction. • Yet, there is little or no software designed specifically to implement the vast array of artistic devices screen printers use to achieve their interpretation of a quality print. The craftsmanship is still a vital element. Designing for this peculiar medium takes a certain familiarity with its limits, and an intuitive and creative sense of compositional and technical engineering to ignore and break these limits. • If this "Tao of the T" has been too much for you, then just turn the page and dig in for yourself.

Colin Cheer, Art Director, Mirror Image, Inc

1
Design Firm: Zedwear
Art Director: John Klaja/George Mimnaugh
Designer: John Klaja/George Mimnaugh
Photographer: Stuart Diekmeyer
Client: Zedwear
Purpose or Occasion: Holiday Retail
Number of Colors: 2
Title: "Spotlight"

2
Design Firm: Zedwear
Art Director: John Klaja/George Mimnaugh
Designer: John Klaja/George Mimnaugh
Illustrator: John Klaja/George Mimnaugh
Client: Zedwear
Purpose or Occasion: Retail
Number of Colors: 5 front/4 back
Title: "Zillion Zeds"

One hundred "Zed" heads on front of the shirt and one on the back of the shirt.

2

1
Design Firm: Sayles Graphic Design
Art Director: John Sayles
Designer: John Sayles
Illustrator: John Sayles
Client: Buena Vista College
Number of Colors: 3/ 1

2
Design Firm: Michael Carr Design
Art Director: Michael Timble/ Propaganda
Designer: Michael Carr
Illustrator: Michael Carr
Client: Ka-Boom!
Purpose or Occasion: Nightclub shirt
Number of Colors: 1

3
Design Firm: Studio MD
Art Director: Glenn Mitsui/Jesse Doquilo/Randy Lim
Illustrator: Glenn Mitsui, Gigi Luk
Client: Colaizzo Opticians
Purpose or Occasion: Retail
Number of Colors: 2

2

3

Beautyware!

2

1
Design Firm: Tilka Design
Art Director: Jane Tilka
Designer: Ann Artz Hadland/Bruce Macindoe
Client: Tilka Design
Purpose or Occasion: Holiday greeting
Number of Colors: 2

2
Design Firm: Marc English: Design
Art Director: Marc English
Client: Theresa Mulvey
Purpose or Occasion: Family Birthday/Anniversary
Number of Colors: 1

Parents are a mathematician and a chemist.

3
Design Firm: Dogfish Design
Art Director: Korey Peterson
Designer: Korey Peterson
Illustrator: Korey Peterson
Purpose or Occasion: Wholesale and retail sale to coffee lovers

3

Number of Colors: 4

T-shirt & sweats come gift wrapped as coffee beans in Italian, French, English, Spanish, Russian, Japanese, German & Greek.

1

2

1
Design Firm: Epstein, Gutzwiller, Schultz & Partners
Art Director: Sylvie Hanna
Designer: Sylvie Hanna
Illustrator: Sylvie Hanna
Client: The Cleveland Orchestra
Purpose or Occasion: Fundraising & Promotion
Number of Colors: 6

2
Design Firm: Sayles Graphic Design
Art Director: John Sayles
Designer: John Sayles
Illustrator: John Sayles
Client: Logo-Motive
Purpose or Occasion: Promotional
Number of Colors: 2

3
Design Firm: Mike Salisbury Communications
Art Director: Mike Salisbury
Designer: Mike Salisbury
Illustrator: Greg Huber
Client: Software Ventures
Purpose or Occasion: Introduce new software
Number of Colors: 6

1

2

TOP DOG

1
Design Firm: Charles S. Anderson Design Co.
Art Director: Charles S. Anderson
Designer: Charles S. Anderson /Daniel Olson
Illustrator: Charles S. Anderson /Randall Dahlk
Client: Cabel Harris/Spy Magazine
Purpose or Occasion: Environmental Action Group
Number of Colors: 6

2
Design Firm: Michael Stanard, Inc.
Art Director: Michael Stanard
Designer: Michael Stanard
Illustrator: Michael Stanard
Client: Michael Stanard, Inc.
Purpose or Occasion: Trademark Parody/Self Promotion
Number of Colors: 1

3
Design Firm: John Evans Design
Art Director: John Evans
Designer: John Evans
Illustrator: John Evans
Purpose or Occasion: Retail
Number of Colors: 2

i'm schizophrenic.
and so am i.

1
Design Firm: John Evans Design
Art Director: John Evans
Designer: John Evans
Illustrator: John Evans
Purpose or Occasion: Retail
Number of Colors: 5

2
Design Firm: Stefan Georg Originals
Designer: Thai Nguyen
Number of Colors: 4

3
Design Firm: Sayles Graphic Design
Art Director: John Sayles
Designer: John Sayles
Illustrator: John Sayles
Client: Villanova University
Purpose or Occasion: Promotion
Number of Colors: 3

A ZONK INC. PRODUCT ©1990 TRACY SABIN

Zonk!

A ZONK INC. PRODUCT ©1989 T.S

Design Firm: Sabin Design
Art Director: Greg Sabin
Designer: Tracy Sabin
Illustrator: Tracy Sabin
Client: Zonk, Inc.
Purpose or Occasion: Retail
Number of Colors: 5

Design Firm: Propaganda Screenprinting
Art Director: Andrew Lucas
Designer: Andrew Lucas
Client: Splat-T's
Purpose or Occasion: Pre-print T-shirt line
Number of Colors: 2

2
Design Firm: Sayles Graphic Design
Art Director: John Sayles
Designer: John Sayles
Illustrator: John Sayles
Client: Drake University
Purpose or Occasion: Direct mail promotion
Number of Colors: 3

3
Design Firm: Fotofolio/Mirror Image
Art Director: Ron Schick
Photographer: Pamela Hanson
Number of Colors: 2

3

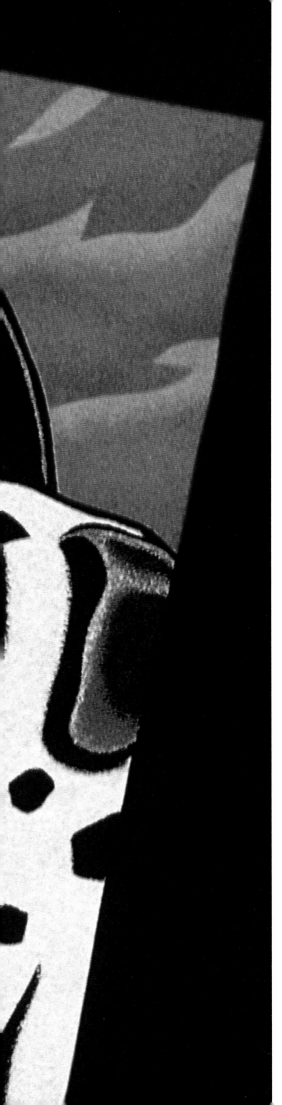

1
Design Firm: Zedwear
Art Director: George Mimnaugh/John Klaja
Designer: George Mimnaugh/John Klaja
Illustrator: Douglas Fraser
Client: Zedwear
Purpose or Occasion: Retail
Number of Colors: 8
Title: "Fire"

2
Design Firm: Michael Stanard, Inc.
Art Director: Michael Stanard
Designer: Michael Stanard
Illustrator: Michael Stanard
Client: Zoological Societies Campaign
Purpose or Occasion: Promotional
Number of Colors: 2

1

2

3

1

Design Firm: Carmichael-Lynch
Art Director: Peter Winecke
Designer: Peter Winecke
Illustrator: Peter Winecke
Client: Minneapolis Lacrosse Club
Purpose or Occasion: Team T-shirt
Number of Colors: 1

Logo designed on the Mac.

2

Design Firm: Punch Design, Inc.
Art Director: Rick Korab
Designer: Rick Korab
Illustrator: Rick Korab
Client: Target Stores
Purpose or Occasion: Honoring kids for their efforts on the environment
Number of Colors: 6

3

Design Firm: Mike Quon Design Office
Art Director: Mike Quon
Designer: Mike Quon
Illustrator: Mike Quon
Client: Mike Quon Design Office
Purpose or Occasion: Self Promotion
Number of Colors: 1

Series photographed all over the world - this shot in African village.

4

Design Firm: Mirror Image/ Electric Eye Studios
Art Director: Rick Roth
Illustrator: Colin J. Cheer
Client: Amnesty International
Number of Colors: 6

Separations created with a copier and zip-a-tone.

4

© 1988 THE ESTATE OF KEITH HARING.

STOP AID

1
Design Firm: Propaganda Screenprinting
Art Director: James Schatz
Illustrator: Keith Haring
Client: Red Hot & Blue
Purpose or Occasion: AIDS fundraising line
Number of Colors: 2

Haring donated this design to "Red Hot & Blue" before he passed away.

2
Design Firm: John Evans Design
Art Director: John Evans
Designer: John Evans
Illustrator: John Evans
Purpose or Occasion: Retail
Number of Colors: 5

2

4

5

1
Design Firm: Michael Stanard, Inc.
Art Director: Lisa Fingerhut
Designer: Marc Fuhrman
Illustrator: Marc Fuhrman
Client: Keep Evanston Beautiful
Purpose or Occasion: Community clean-up event
Number of Colors: 3

2
Design Firm: Punch Design, Inc.
Art Director: Rick Korab
Designer: Rick Korab
Illustrator: Rick Korab
Client: Nice Man Merchandising
Purpose or Occasion: Men's crew sportswear
Number of Colors: 5

3
Design Firm: Creative Arts Group
Art Director: Gaylord Bennitt
Designer: Gaylord Bennittt
Illustrator: Gaylord Bennitt
Client: Rennie O'Brien Presents
Purpose or Occasion: Rugby season at Kezar
Number of Colors: 4

Rugby 'Players' with apologies to Leyendeurer.

4
Design Firm: Sommese Design
Art Director: Lanny Sommese
Designer: Lanny Sommese
Illustrator: Lanny Sommese
Client: Central Pennsylvania Festival of the Arts
Purpose or Occasion: Annual Summer Festival of the Visual and Performing Arts
Number of Colors: 2

5
Design Firm: Sayles Graphic Design
Art Director: John Sayles
Designer: John Sayles
Illustrator: John Sayles
Client: Drake University
Purpose or Occasion: Promotional
Number of Colors: 5

1

2

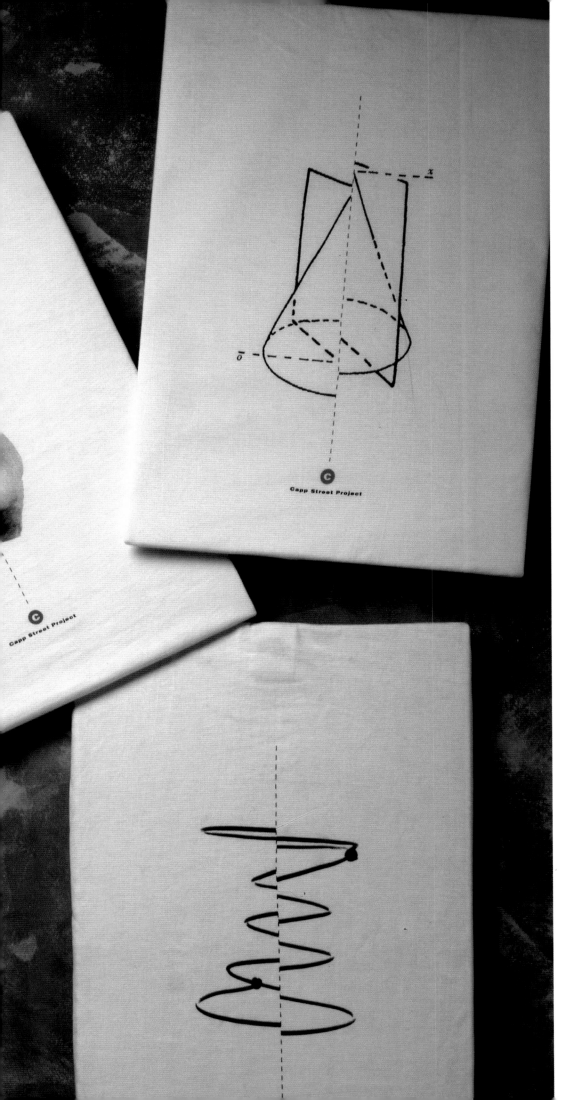

1
Design Firm: The Pushpin Group
Art Director: Seymour Chwast
Designer: Roxanne Slimak
Client: Rudy Mosley/Telephone Bar & Grill
Number of Colors: 3

2
Design Firm: Sommese Design
Art Director: Kristin Sommese
Designer: Jim Lilly
Illustrator: Jim Lilly
Client: Penn State Intra-Fraternity Council
Purpose or Occasion: 20th Anniversary Dance
Marathon Charity
Number of Colors: 4

Proceeds benefit children with cancer.

3
Design Firm: Morla Design
Art Director: Jennifer Morla
Designer: Jennifer Morla/Sharrie Brooks
Illustrator: Holly Stewart
Client: Capp Street Project
Number of Colors: 2

1
Design Firm: Segura Inc.
Art Director: Carlos Segura
Designer: Carlos Segura
Illustrator: Mary Flock Lempa
Client: The Chicago Lung Association Distance Classic
Purpose or Occasion: Promotional
Number of Colors: 2

2
Design Firm: Carmichael-Lynch
Art Director: Peter Winecke
Designer: Peter Winecke
Illustrator: Peter Winecke
Client: Minnesota Illiteracy Council
Purpose or Occasion: Promotion with Minnesota Twins
"Strike out Illiteracy"
Number of Colors: 4

Logo designed on Mac.

3
Design Firm: Sibley/ Peteet Design
Art Director: Tim Robbinson
Designer: Tim Robbinson
Illustrator: Tim Robbinson
Client: Texas AIGA
Purpose or Occasion: Computer conference
Number of Colors: 5

4

1

2

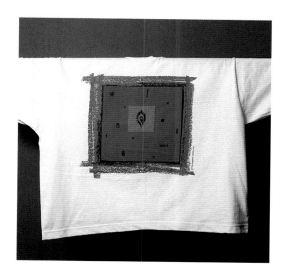

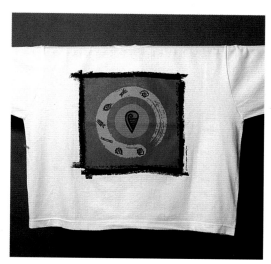

1
Design Firm: Aardvark Studio
Illustrator: Andy Lackow
Client: Mega Designs
Purpose or Occasion: Retail

2
Design Firm: Pictogram Studio
Art Director: Stephanie Hooton
Designer: Hien Nguyen/Stephanie Hooton
Illustrator: Stephanie Hooton
Client: Pictogram Studio
Purpose or Occasion: Self Promotion
Number of Colors: 4

1

1
Design Firm: Vaughn/ Wedeen Creative, Inc.
Art Director: Dan Flynn
Designer: Dan Flynn
Illustrator: Dan Flynn/ Bill Gerhold
Client: Jones Intercable
Purpose or Occasion: New campaign kick-off
Number of Colors: 6

2
Design Firm: Carmichael-Lynch
Art Director: Peter Winecke
Designer: Peter Winecke
Illustrator: Peter Winecke
Client: General Growth
Purpose or Occasion: Conference on retailing in
the year 2000
Number of Colors: 3

2

2

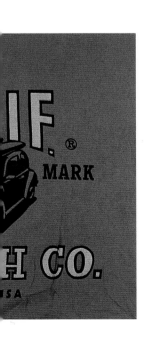

3

1
Design Firm: Hornall Anderson Design Works
Art Director: Jack Anderson, Julia LaPine
Designer: Jack Anderson/Julia LaPine/Denise Weir/Lian Ng
Illustrator: Larry Jost
Client: Puget Sound Marketing Corporation
Purpose or Occasion: New identity application
Number of Colors: 4

2
Design Firm: Sibley/Peteet Design
Art Director: John Evans
Designer: John Evans
Illustrator: John Evans
Client: Sibley/Peteet Design
Purpose or Occasion: Annual Chili Cookoff
Number of Colors: 3

3
Design Firm: Sabin Design
Art Director: Richard Sawyer
Designer: Tracy Sabin
Illustrator: Tracy Sabin
Client: California Beach Co.
Purpose or Occasion: Retail

1
Design Firm: Sibley/Peteet Design
Art Director: Rex Peteet
Designer: Rex Peteet
Illustrator: Rex Peteet
Client: Uptown Express
Purpose or Occasion: Bicycle delivery service
Number of Colors: 3

2
Design Firm: Carmichael-Lynch
Art Director: Peter Winecke
Designer: Peter Winecke
Illustrator: Peter Winecke
Client: CLX
Purpose or Occasion: New business
Number of Colors: 4

Illustration created on the Mac.

3
Design Firm: Michael Stanard, Inc.
Art Director: Marcos Chavez
Designer: Mark Naden
Client: Millenium
Purpose of Occasion: Retail
Number of Colors: 1

1
Design Firm: KaiserDicken
Art Director: Debra Kaiser
Designer: Debra Kaiser
Illustrator: Debra Kaiser
Client: Black Sheep Woolens
Purpose or Occasion: Company T-shirt
Number of Colors: 1

2
Design Firm: KaiserDicken
Art Director: Craig Dicken/Debra Kaiser
Designer: Craig Dicken/Debra Kaiser
Illustrator: Craig Dicken
Client: Sailworks
Purpose or Occasion: Regatta "Summers End"
Number of Colors: 3

3
Design Firm: The Graphic Design Office of Jim Vandegrift
Art Director: Jim Vandegrift
Designer: Jim Vandegrift
Client: Annie Glass Studio
Purpose or Occasion: Trade Show
Number of Colors: 2

3

1

1991 Dallas YMCA

TURKEY TROT

2

EVANS FAMILY REUNION

AUGUST 1991

3

1993 FORT WORTH
COWTOWN
MARATHON & 10K

1
Design Firm: Dally Advertising
Art Director: Randy Padorr-Black
Designer: Randy Padorr-Black
Illustrator: Randy Padorr-Black
Client: Downtown Dallas YMCA
Purpose or Occasion: 10K Run/Thanksgiving Day
Number of Colors: 6
Printer: Silverwing Productions, Dallas, TX

2
Design Firm: Leslie Evans Illustration
Art Director: Leslie Evans
Designer: Leslie Evans
Illustrator: Leslie Evans
Client: Evans Family
Purpose or Occasion: Evans family reunion
Number of Colors: 3

Linocut portrait of family patriarch, wood type
used for words.

3
Design Firm: Dally Advertising
Art Director: Randy Padorr-Black
Designer: Randy Padorr-Black
Illustrator: Randy Padorr-Black
Client: Cowtown Marathon
Purpose or Occasion: Marathon & 10K Run
Number of Colors: 6
Printer: Lonestar Sportswear, Fort Worth, TX

2

3

Design Firm: The Bennitt Group
Art Director: Dave Dittman
Designer: Gaylord Bennitt
Illustrator: Gaylord Bennitt
Client: Mike Pinto
Purpose or Occasion: Promotional
Number of Colors: 6

Water based ink - no solvents.

2

Design Firm: Richard Fish Associates
Art Director: Richard Fish
Designer: Richard Rish
Illustrator: Richard Fish
Client: Valley Forge Park Interpretive Association
Purpose or Occasion: 100th Anniversary of Valley
Forge Park
Number of Colors: 1

3

Design Firm: Electric Design
Art Director: Joette Spinelli
Designer: Joette Spinelli
Illustrator: Edward Evanisko
Client: Colgate-Palmolive Company
Purpose or Occasion: Citywide Shadow Day/ Logo identity
Number of Colors: 4

Prepared on the Mac in the Adobe Illustrator Program.

4

Design Firm: Bright & Associates
Art Director: Konrad Bright
Designer: Konrad Bright
Illustrator: Konrad Bright
Client: Los Angeles Advertising
Purpose or Occasion: Softball league
Number of Colors: 5

Design Firm: John Evans Design
Art Director: John Evans
Designer: John Evans
Illustrator: John Evans
Purpose or Occasion: Children's retail

Parrot, Penguin, Rooster

1

2

1
Design Firm: Sabin Design
Art Director: Bobby Grillo/John Goldsmith
Designer: Tracy Sabin
Illustrator: Tracy Sabin
Client: California Blues
Purpose or Occasion: Retail

2
Design Firm: The Riordon Design Group Inc.
Art Director: Ric Riordon
Designer: Ric Riordon
Illustrator: Glenn Tait
Client: Van Gosh Decorating Ltd.
Purpose or Occasion: Employees attire for working on site
Number of Colors: 2

Computer-generated artwork.

3
Design Firm: John Evans Design
Art Director: John Evans
Designer: John Evans
Illustrator: John Evans
Client: Adrian Ray
Purpose or Occasion: Retail
Number of Colors: 5

3

THE WEARABLE-ART GALLERY
DEEP ELLUM, TEXAS

a confused & often demented state of mind induced by the tropics

TROPO

Design Firm: Sabin Design
Art Director: Bobby Grillo/John Goldsmith
Designer: Tracy Sabin
Illustrator: Tracy Sabin
Client: Tropo
Purpose or Occasion: Retail

4

1

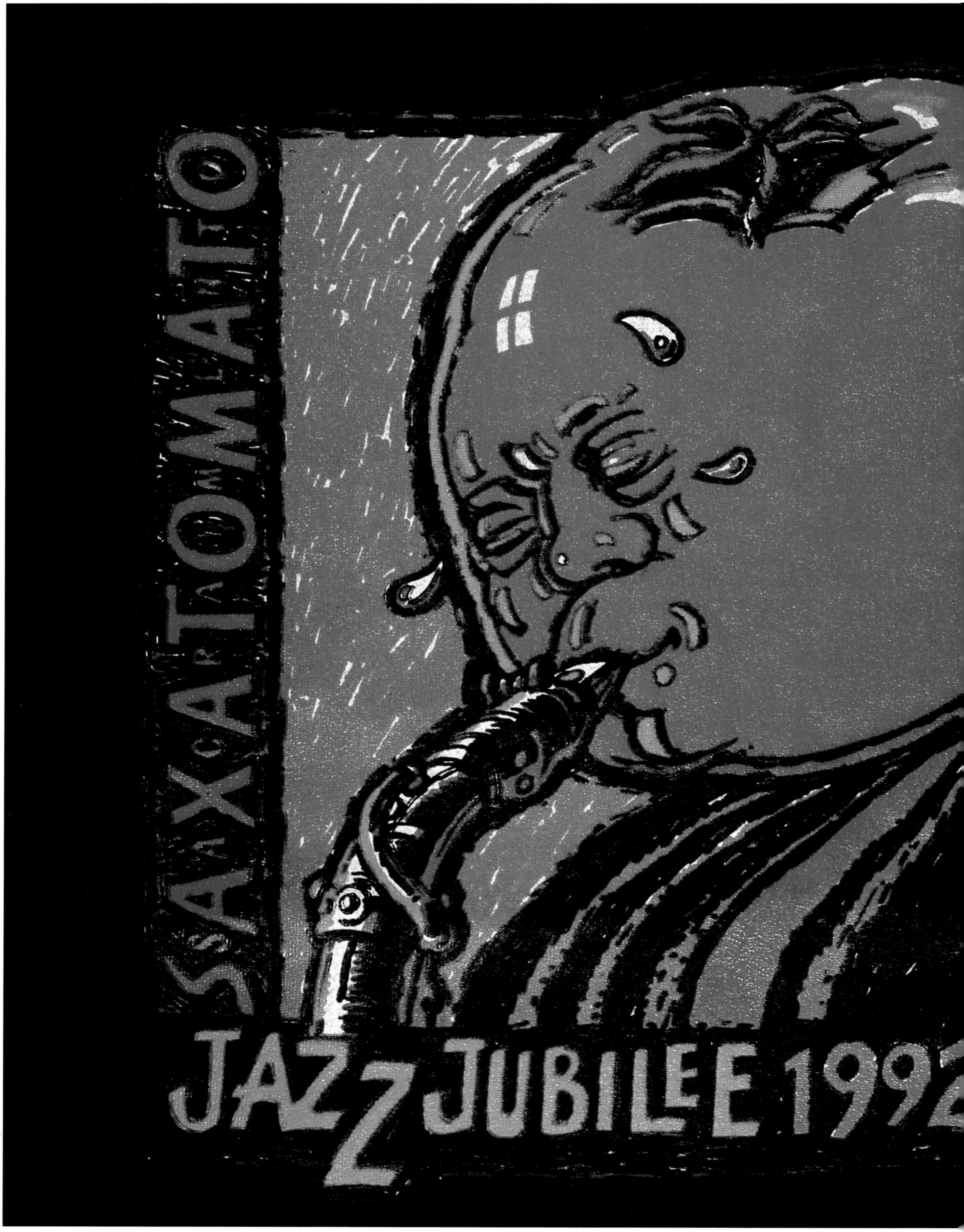

1
Design Firm: Creative Arts Group
Art Director: Gaylord Bennitt
Designer: Gaylord Bennitt
Illustrator: Gaylord Bennitt
Client: Sacramento Traditional Jazz Society
Purpose or Occasion: Sacramento Jazz Jubilee 1992
Number of Colors: 6
Title: Metamorphoses

2
Design Firm: Vaughn/Wedeen Creative, Inc.
Art Director: Rick Vaughn
Designer: Rick Vaughn
Illustrator: Rick Vaughn
Client: Duke City Marathon
Purpose or Occasion: Duke City Marathon
Number of Colors: 4

2

1

2

3

4

5

NEW ENGLAND AQUARIU
BOSTON, MASS.

6

1
Design Firm: Michael Stanard, Inc.
Art Director: Lisa Fingerhut
Designer: Michael Stanard
Illustrator: Michael Stanard
Client: Michael Stanard, Inc.
Purpose or Occasion: Trademark Parody/Self Promotion
Number of Colors: 3

2
Design Firm: Cyrk
Art Director: Dave Saltonstall
Designer: Dave Saltonstall
Client: Cyrk Retail

Print & Embroidery

3
Design Firm: Vaughn/Wedeen Creative Inc.
Art Director: Rick Vaughn
Designer: Rick Vaughn
Illustrator: Rick Vaughn
Client: The Santa Fe Opera
Purpose or Occasion: Intern T-shirt
Number of Colors: 4

4
Design Firm: Cyrk, Inc.
Art Director: Heidi Reardon
Designer: Heidi Reardon
Client: Willis & Geiger
Purpose or Occasion: Vintage Aircraft Series
Number of Colors: 7

5
Design Firm: Cyrk, Inc.
Art Director: Stephanie Moore
Designer: Stephanie Moore
Illustrator: Stephanie Moore
Client: New England Aquarium
Purpose or Occasion: Promotional
Number of Colors: 8

6
Design Firm: Michael Stanard, Inc.
Art Director: Marcos Chavez
Designer: Mark Naden/Marcos Chavez
Illustrator: Mark Naden
Client: Millenium
Purpose or Occasion: Retail
Number of Colors: 1

1

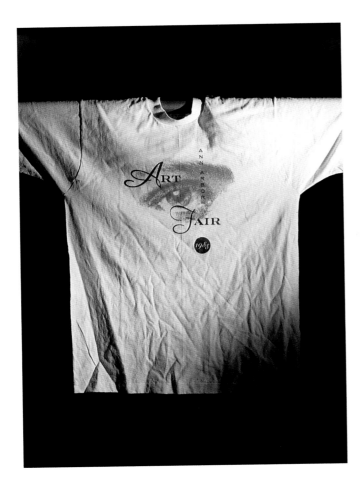

2

WILL

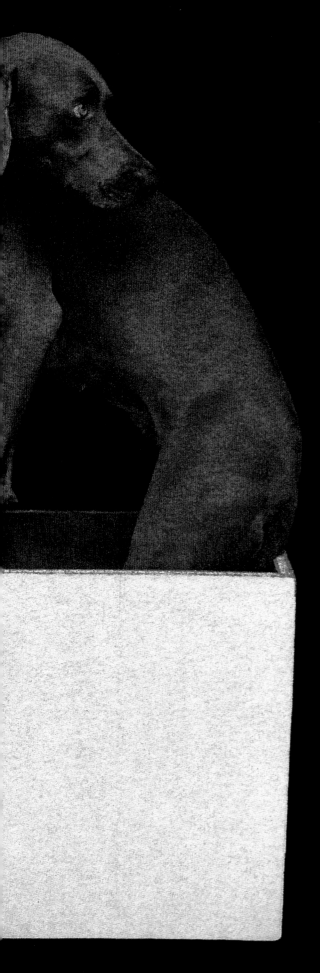

E BOX, 1987. © WILLIAM WEGMAN. FOTOFOLIO EDITIONS

AM WEGMAN

1
Design Firm: Visual Dialogue
Art Director: Paul Montie/Fritz Klaetke
Designer: Paul Montie/Fritz Klaetke
Illustrator: Paul Montie/Fritz Klaetke
Client: Visual Dialogue
Purpose or Occasion: Ann Arbor Art Fair
Number of Colors: 2

The "Eye" looks at you from 100 paces.

2
Design Firm: Visual Dialogue
Art Director: Fritz Klaetke
Designer: Fritz Klaetke
Client: Cell & Development Biology Program,
Harvard Medical School
Purpose or Occasion: Softball Team
Number of Colors: 2

Barnovsky is a former chairman of the program.

3
Design Firm: Fotofolio/Mirror Image
Art Director: Ron Schick
Photographer: Original photo by William Wegman
Client: Fotofolio
Number of Colors: 4

1

1
Design Firm: Morla Design
Art Director: Jennifer Morla
Designer: Jennifer Morla
Illustrator: Jennifer Morla
Client: ESPRIT De Corp.
Purpose or Occasion: Designed as ESPRIT's contribution
of exclusive T-shirts for Bloomingdales' "California"
promotion
Number of Colors: 5

2
Design Firm: Visual Dialogue
Art Director: Fritz Klaetke
Designer: Fritz Klaetke
Client: Enuffa-My-Butt Productions
Purpose or Occasion: Chucklehead's "Big Wet Kiss" Tour
Number of Colors: 4

3
Design Firm: Pictogram Studios
Art Director: Stephanie Hooton
Designer: Hien Nguyen/ Stephanie Hooton
Illustrator: Hien Nguyen
Client: Pictogram Studio
Purpose or Occasion: Self Promotion
Number of Colors: 2

The year of the monkey.

3

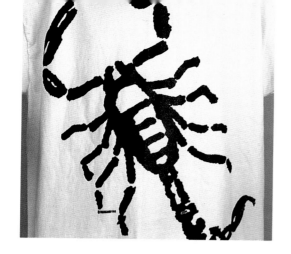

Design Firm: Propaganda Screenprinting
Art Director: Jeff Heller
Designer: Jeff Heller
Illustrator: Jeff Heller
Client: Gene Chaney/ Propaganda
Purpose or Occasion: Custom pre-print "Big Bug" line
Number of Colors: 1

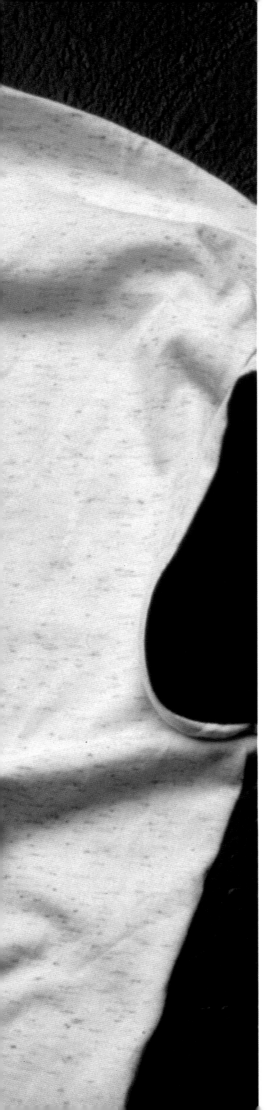

1
Design Firm: Sayles Graphic Design
Art Director: John Sayles
Designer: John Sayles
Illustrator: John Sayles
Client: Central Life Assurance
Purpose or Occasion: Gift
Number of Colors: 3

2
Design Firm: Paper Shrine
Art Director: Paul Dean
Designer: Paul Dean
Illustrator: (apologies to) Albrecht Durer
Client: Barefoot Press, Raleigh N.C.
Purpose or Occasion: Promotional
Number of Colors: 2

2

MYSTERY!

For those unforgettable evenings...

CHANNEL
Nº2

W   G   B   H   TV

LAST
Garage
CHANCE

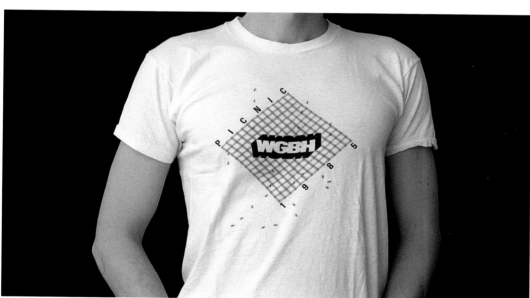

4

1
Design Firm: WGBH Design
Art Director: Chris Pullman
Designer: Chris Pullman
Illustrator: Mark Fisher
Client: MYSTERY!/ WGBH
Number of Colors: 2

2
Design Firm: WGBH Design
Art Director: Chris Pullman
Designer: Chris Pullman
Photo: Tom Sumida
Number of Colors: 2

3
Design Firm: WGBH Design
Art Director: Chris Pullman
Designer: Chris Pullman
Logo Design: Gene Mackles
Client: Last Chance Garage/ WGBH
Number of Colors: 4

5

4
Design Firm: WGBH Design
Art Director: Chris Pullman
Designer: Chris Pullman
Client: Ice Cream Fun Fest
Number of Colors: 5

5
Design Firm: WGBH Design
Art Director: Paul Souza
Designer: Mary Salvadore
Client: WGBH Picnic
Number of Colors: 2

6
Design Firm: WGBH Design
Art Director: Alison Kennedy
Designer: Elles Gianocostas
Photo: Arizona Historical Society
Client: The American Experience/ WGBH
Number of Colors: 4

6

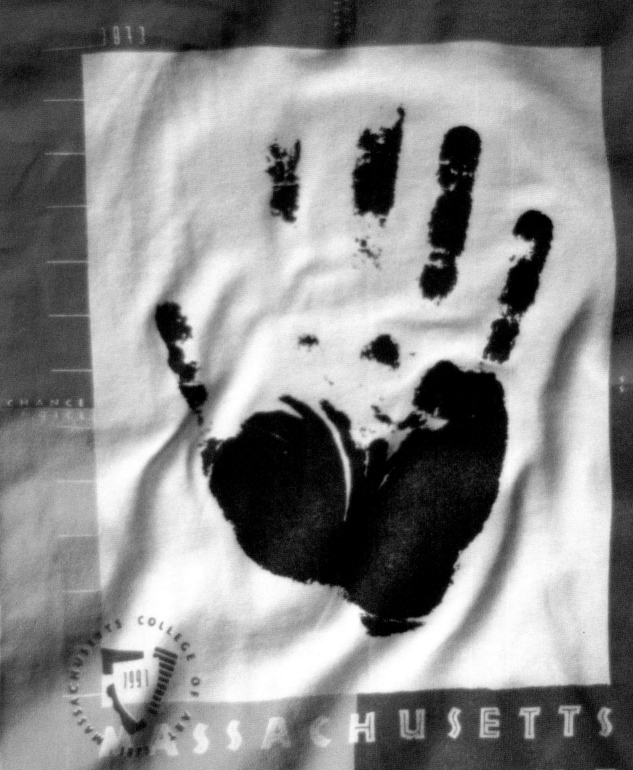

MASSACHUSETTS
COLLEGE OF ART

1
Design Firm: Marc English: Design
Designer: Marc English
Client: Massachusetts College of Art
Purpose or Occasion: Fundraising premium
Number of Colors: 5

2
Design Firm: Visual Dialogue
Art Director: Fritz Klaetke/Paul Montie
Designer: Fritz Klaetke/Paul Montie
Illustrator: Fritz Klaetke/Paul Montie
Client: Eclipse Jazz
Purpose or Occasion: Ann Arbor Art Fair
Number of Colors: 2

3
Design Firm: Cyrk, Inc.
Art Director: Tom Gardner
Designer: Tom Gardner
Illustrator: Tom Gardner
Client: Cyrk Retail
Number of Colors: 5

3

1

2

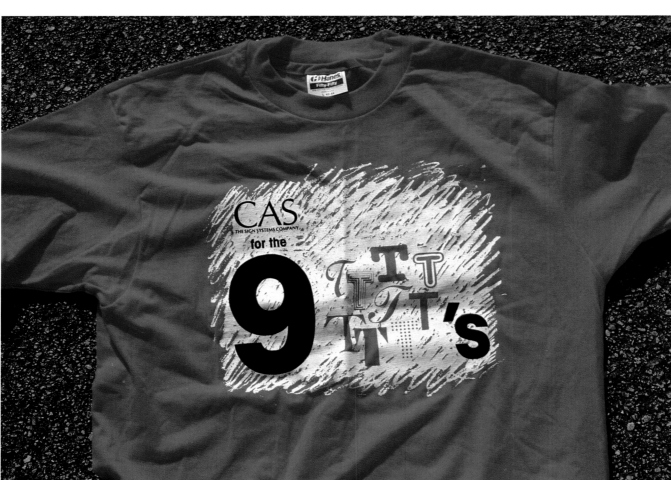

1
Design Firm: Judi Radice Design Consultant
Art Director: Judi Radice
Designer: Bruce Yelaska
Photographer: Beatrice Coll
Client: Heartwise Express Restaurant
Purpose or Occassion: Promotional
Number of Colors: 1

2
Design Firm: CAS The Sign Systems Company
Art Director: David Rothstein
Designer: Arno Ford Furstenberg/Frank
Blesch/David Luther
Client: Self Promotion
Purpose or Occasion: Holiday giveaway

3
Design Firm: Sommese Design
Art Director: Lanny Sommese
Designer: Lanny Sommese
Illustrator: Lanny Sommese
Client: Central Pennsylvania Festival of the Arts
Purpose or Occasion: Annual Summer Festival for the
Visual and Performing Arts
Number of Colors: 4

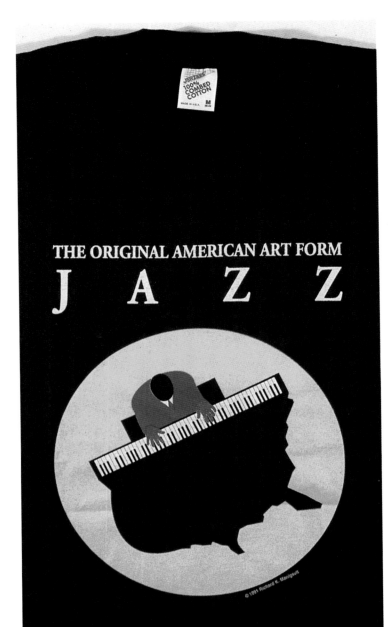

4

BACK IN TIME

Swatch

GUARNACCIA

1
Design Firm: Gardner Design
Art Director: Nancy Gardner
Designer: Joel Templin
Illustrator: Joel Templin
Client: Minnesota Special Olympics
Purpose or Occasion: Volunteer shirt for Fall Sports Classic
Number of Colors: 4

2
Design Firm: Manigault Design
Art Director: Richard K. Manigault
Designer: Richard K. Manigault
Illustrator: Richard K. Manigault
Client: Manigault Design
Purpose or Occasion: Self Promotion and Retail
Number of Colors: 4

3
Design Firm: Sayles Graphic Design
Art Director: John Sayles
Designer: John Sayles
Illustrator: John Sayles
Client: Advertising Professionals of Des Moines
Purpose or Occasion: 25th Anniversary ADDY Awards
Number of Colors: 2

4
Art Director: Cheryl Chung
Designer: Steven Guarnaccia
Illustrator: Steven Guarnaccia
Client: Swatch
Purpose or Occasion: Promotional
Number of Colors: 5

1
Design Firm: Charles S. Anderson Design Co.
Art Director: Daniel Olson / Charles S. Anderson
Designer: Charles S. Anderson / Daniel Olson
Illustrator: Daniel Olson / Kobe
Client: AIGA Minnesota
Purpose or Occasion: Annual design camp
Number of Colors: 4

2
Design Firm: Sabin Design
Art Director: Richard Sawyer
Designer: Tracy Sabin
Illustrator: Tracy Sabin
Client: California Beach Co.
Purpose or Occasion: Retail
Number of Colors: 11

T-shirt was triple printed.

2

1

2

3

1
Design Firm: Fotofolio/ Mirror Image Inc.
Art Director: Ron Schick
Photographer: James Van Der Zee (Original Photo)
Number of Colors: 4
Printer: Mirror Image, Inc.

2
Design Firm: Sibley/ Peteet Design
Art Director: John Evans
Designer: John Evans
Illustrator: John Evans
Client: Sibley/ Peteet Design
Purpose or Occasion: Annual Chili Cookoff
Number of Colors: 3

3
Design Firm: John Evans Design
Art Director: John Evans
Designer: John Evans
Illustrator: John Evans
Client: Jeff Veverka
Purpose or Occasion: Softball team
Number of Colors: 1

4
Design Firm: Reactor
Art Director: Louise Fishauf
Designer: Steven Guarnaccia
Illustrator: Steven Guarnaccia
Client: Reactor Art & Design
Purpose or Occasion: Promotional
Number of Colors: 5

5
Design Firm: Pictogram Studio
Art Director: Stephanie Hooton
Designer: Hien Nguyen/Stephanie Hooton
Illustrator: Hien Hguyen
Client: Pictogram Studio
Purpose or Occasion: Self Promotion
Number of Colors: 1

Celerbrates the year of the ram.

1

2

FisH out of Wate

1
Design Firm: Sibley/Peteet
Art Director: Rex Peteet/Supon Phornirunlit
Designer: Rex Peteet
Illustrator: Rex Peteet
Client: International Logos and Trademarks
(Supon Design Group)
Purpose or Occasion: T-shirt for judges
Number of Colors: 10

2
Design Firm: Letvin Design
Designer: Carolyn Letvin
Illustrator: Carolyn Letvin
Client: PC Week Magazine
Purpose or Occasion: Conference giveaway
Number of Colors: 4

3
Design Firm: John Evans Design
Art Director: John Evans
Designer: John Evans
Illustrator: John Evans
Purpose or Occasion: Retail
Number of Colors: 4

CREATE A SCENE

THE SANTA FE OPERA

1

1
Design Firm: Vaughn/Wedeen Creative, Inc.
Art Director: Rick Vaughn
Designer: Rick Vaughn
Client: The Sante Fe Opera
Purpose or Occasion: Retail
Number of Colors: 4

2
Design Firm: Art Guy Studios
Art Director: James F. Kraus
Designer: James F. Kraus
Illustrator: James F. Kraus
Client: Art Guy Studios
Purpose or Occasion: Self Promotion
Number of Colors: 1

3
Design Firm: Ted Hansen Design Associates
Art Director: Ten Hansen
Designer: Ted Hansen
Illustrator: Ted Hansen
Client: Ted Hansen Design Associates
Purpose or Occasion: THDA's 20th Anniversary
Number of Colors: 6

3

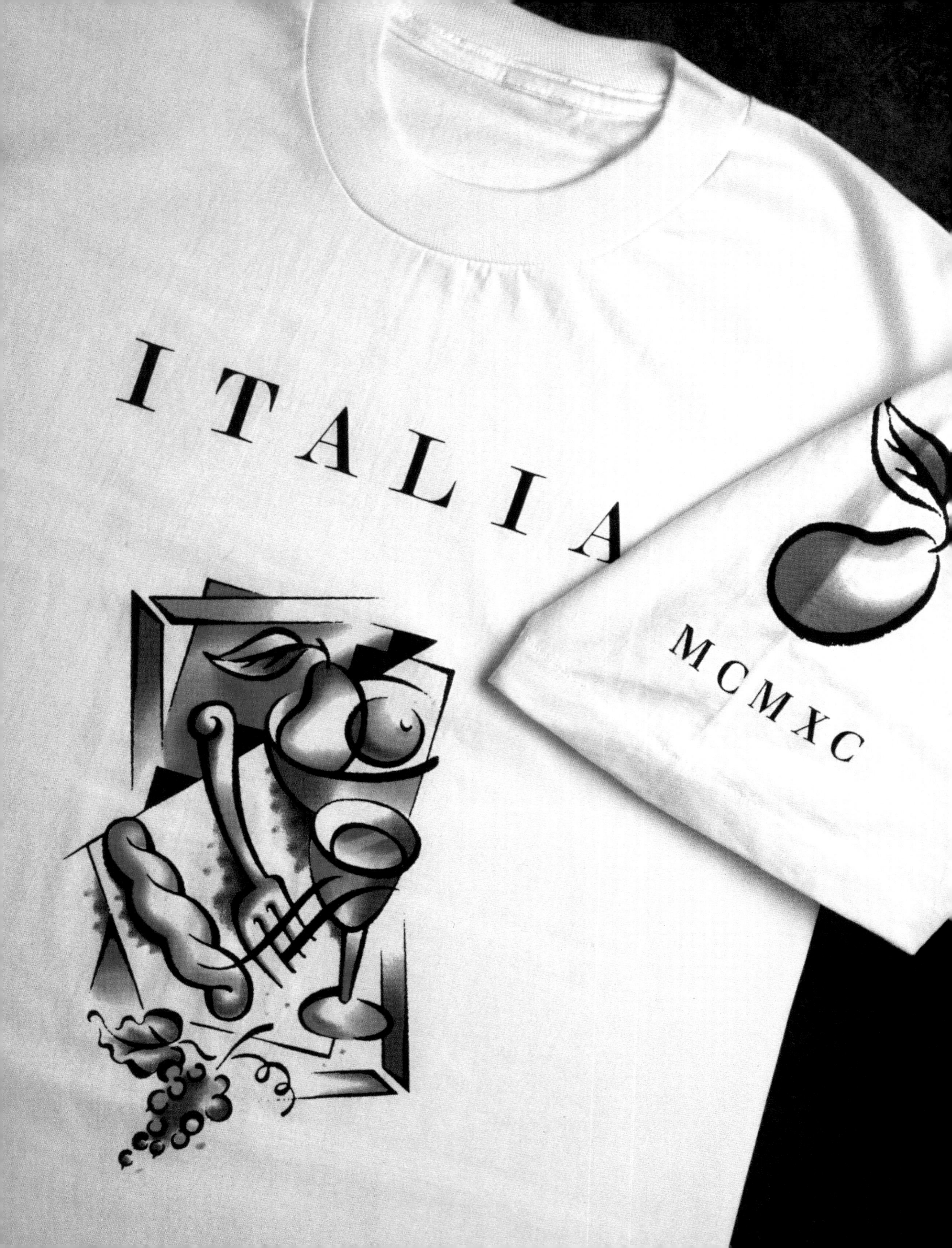

ITALIA
MCMXC

Design Firm: Hornall Anderson Design Works, Inc.
Art Director: Jack Anderson
Designer: Jack Anderson/Julia LaPine
Illustrator: Julia LaPine
Client: Italia
Purpose or Occasion: Promotional
Number of Colors: 4

T-shirt is worn by employees and is for sale to customers.

Design Firm: Conge Design
Art Director: Sue Kemp
Designer: Bob Conge
Illustrator: Bob Conge
Client: Screen Machine U.S.A.
Purpose or Occasion: Retail
Number of Colors: 4
Printer: Screen Machine U.S.A., Rochester, NY

1

2

3

4

5

6

1
Design Firm: Zedwear
Art Director: John Klaja/George Mimnaugh
Designer: John Klaja/George Mimnaugh
Illustrator: Steve Vance
Client: Zedwear
Purpose or Occasion: Retail
Number of Colors: 5
Title: "Spot Remover"

2
Design Firm: Sommese Design
Art Director: Lanny Sommese
Designer: Lanny Sommese
Illustrator: Lanny Sommese
Client: Penn State University
Purpose or Occasion: Conference
Number of Colors: 3

Shirt was given to conference participants and later sold to the public.

3
Design Firm: Gunnar Swanson Design Office
Art Director: Gunnar Swanson
Designer: Gunnar Swanson
Illustrator: Gunnar Swanson
Client: C.A. Singer & Associates
Number of Colors: 2

4
Design Firm: Pictogram Studio
Art Director: Stephanie Hooton
Designer: Hien Nguyen/Stephanie Hooton
Illustrator: Stephanie Hooton
Client: Pictogram Studio
Purpose or Occasion: Self Promotion
Number of Colors: 3
Title: "Which comes first - egg or chicken?"

5
Design Firm: Cyrk
Art Director: Heidi Reardon
Designer: Heidi Reardon
Client: British Khaki
Purpose or Occasion: Retail
Number of Colors: 6

6
Design Firm: Amber Productions, Inc.
Art Director: Noel A. Traver
Designer: Todd Mock/John Garrison
Client: D'pix, Inc.
Purpose or Occasion: Shirt used for software packaging
Number of Colors: 7

Shirt wraps around software ("softwear") replacing the need for a box.

Design Firm: John Evans Design
Art Director: John Evans
Designer: John Evans
Illustrator: John Evans
Client: Replicator
Purpose or Occasion: Retail
Number of Colors: Various

Deep Ellum is an artsy section of Dallas with restaurants,
club and shops.

SAN FRANCISCO BREWING COMPANY™

FROM GRAIN to GLASS

B
I
G
G

1
Design Firm: Lance Anderson Design
Art Director: Lance Anderson
Designer: Lance Anderson
Illustrator: Lance Anderson
Client: San Francisco Brewing Company
Purpose or Occasion: Promotional
Number of Colors: 4

2
Design Firm: Lines 3 Design
Designer: Eric Behrenfeld
Client: Bigg Gear
Purpose or Occasion: Retail

3
Design Firm: Ed the Dog Productions
Art Director: Jeff Schuetz
Designer: Wayne Joplin
Illustrator: Jeff Schuetz
Purpose or Occasion: To have fun
Number of Colors: 1

3

ed the dog

The Garden

Design Firm: John Evans Design
Art Director: John Evans
Designer: John Evans
Illustrator: John Evans
Purpose or Occasion: Retail
Number of Colors: 1

1
Art Director: Steven Guarnaccia
Designer: Steven Guarnaccia
Illustrator: Steven Guarnaccia
Client: 10-S
Purpose or Occasion: Promotional
Number of Colors: 6

2
Design Firm: Sayles Graphic Design
Art Director: John Sayles
Designer: John Sayles
Illustrator: John Sayles
Client: Schaffer's Tuxedo Express
Purpose or Occasion: Gift
Number of Colors: 1

2

1

2

3

BROOKLANDS COLLEGE LIBRARY
WEYBRIDGE, SURREY KT13 8TT

1
Art Director: Melinda Beck
Designer: Melinda Beck
Illustrator: Melinda Beck
Client: Quicksand
Purpose or Occasion: Promotional
Number of Colors: 4

2
Design Firm: Sabin Design
Art Director: Richard Sawyer
Designer: Tracy Sabin
Illustrator: Tracy Sabin
Client: California Beach Co.
Purpose or Occasion: Retail
Number of Colors: 3

3
Design Firm: Sabin Design
Art Director: Greg Sabin
Designer: Tracy Sabin
Illustrator: Tracy Sabin
Client: Kamikaze Skate
Purpose or Occasion: Retail
Number of Colors: 2

4
Design Firm: John Evans Design
Art Director: John Evans
Designer: John Evans
Illustrator: John Evans
Client: Nedley's Bar & Grill
Purpose or Occasion: Basketball tournament
Number of Colors: 2

5
Design Firm: Sabin Design
Art Director: Bobby Grillo/John Goldsmith
Designer: Tracy Sabin
Illustrator: Tracy Sabin
Client: California Blues
Purpose or Occasion: Retail
Number of Colors: 5

2

Design Firm: Pear Graphics
Art Director: Mike Wesko
Designer: Kim A. Farnham
Illustrator: Kim A. Farnham
Client: Pear Graphics, Inc.
Purpose or Occasion: Self Promotion
Number of Colors: 4

2

Design Firm: THARP DID IT
Art Director: Rick Tharp
Designer: Rick Tharp
Illustrator: Jean Mogannam
Client: Belch Computers
Purpose or Occasion: Employee Ts
Number of Colors: 3

3

Design Firm: Temel West Inc.
Art Director: Roy DeYoung
Designer: Chris Blakeman
Illustrator: Chris Blakeman
Client: Idaho Shakespeare Festival
Purpose or Occasion: Promotional
Number of Colors: 4

3

1

2

1
Design Firm: Hornall Anderson Design Works Inc.
Art Director: Jack Anderson
Designer: Jack Anderson/Julia LaPine/David Bates
Illustrator: Hornall Anderson Design Works
Client: Active Voice
Purpose or Occasion: New identity
Number of Colors: 2

2
Design Firm: Sayles Graphic Design
Art Director: John Sayles
Designer: John Sayles
Illustrator: John Sayles
Client: Schaffer's Bridal Shop
Purpose or Occasion: Gift
Number of Colors: 1

3
Design Firm: Musikar Design
Art Director: Sharon R. Musikar
Designer: Sharon R. Musikar
Illustrator: Sharon R. Musikar
Client: The Barrie School
Purpose or Occasion: Annual school T-shirt
Number of Colors: 6

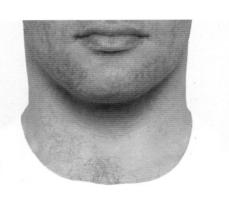

1

2

3

1
Design Firm: Micrografx Creative Services Group
Art Director: Karen J. Smith
Illustrator: Karen J. Smith
Client: Micrografx Inc.
Purpose or Occasion: "Olympic" Theme
Tradeshow Giveaway
Number of Colors: 5

Entirely created and color separated on computer using
Micrografx Designer Software.

2
Design Firm: Mike Quon Design Office
Art Director: Alene Loeser
Designer: Mike Quon
Illustrator: Mike Quon
Client: American Health
Purpose or Occasion: Promotional
Number of Colors: 7

3
Design Firm: Zedwear
Art Director: John Klaja
Designer: John Klaja
Illustrator: John Klaja
Client: Zedwear
Purpose or Occasion: Retail
Number of Colors: 2
Title: "Classic Zed"

Dog wraps around side of shirt.

4
Design Firm: Charles S. Anderson Design Co.
Art Director: Charles S. Anderson
Designer: Daniel Olson / Charles S. Anderson
Illustrator: Charles S. Anderson / Daniel Olson
Client: Minneapolis College of Art & Design
Purpose or Occasion: New Identity Program
Number of Colors: 3

1
Design Firm: Charles S. Anderson Design Co.
Art Director: Charles S. Anderson
Designer: Charles S. Anderson/Daniel Olson
Illustrator: Daniel Olson/Randall Dahlk
Client: Jerry French
Purpose or Occasion: Elementary School Logo
Number of Colors: 1

2
Design Firm: Tilka Design
Art Director: Jane Tilka
Designer: Jane Tilka
Illustrator: Jane Tilka
Client: Tilka Design
Purpose or Occasion: Holiday greeting
Number of Colors: 6

Fishing for Northern Pike ("Snakes")

3
Design Firm: Propaganda Screenprinting
Art Director: Daniel Klingelsmith
Designer: Daniel Klingelsmith
Illustrator: Daniel Klingelsmith
Client: Propaganda
Purpose or Occasion: Self Promotion
Number of Colors: 1

4
Design Firm: Real Impressions
Art Director: Patrick Thompson
Designer: Patrick Thompson
Illustrator: Patrick Thompson
Client: Snake Cup Challenge
Purpose or Occasion: Annual Fishing Trip to Canada
Number of Colors: 5

Design Firm: Sergio Illustration Design
Art Director: Sergio Igartua
Designer: Sergio Igartua
Illustrator: Sergio Igartua
Client: JMR Apparel Marketing
Purpose or Occasion: Retail
Number of Colors: 4

1

2

3

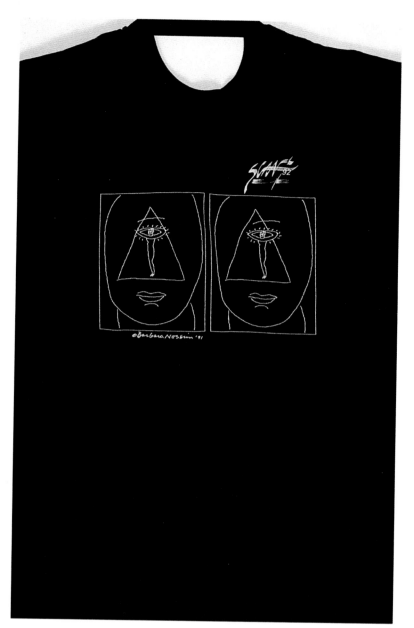

1
Design Firm: Art Guy Studios
Art Director: James F. Kraus
Designer: James F. Kraus
Illustrator: James F. Kraus
Client: WZBC 90.3 FM
Purpose or Occasion: Pledge Premium
Number of Colors: 1

2
Design Firm: John Evans Design
Art Director: John Evans
Designer: John Evans
Illustrator: John Evans
Client: Adrian Ray
Purpose or Occasion: Retail and promotional
Number of Colors: 4

3
Design Firm: Sayles Graphic Design
Art Director: John Sayles
Designer: John Sayles
Illustrator: John Sayles
Client: University of California, Berkeley
Purpose or Occasion: Promotion
Number of Colors: 3

4
Art Director: Misako
Designer: Misako
Illustrator: Barbara Nessim
Client: T-shirt for SCAN Conference (Small Computers in the Arts Network)
Purpose or Occasion: Computer art conference
Number of Colors: 1

Art is 3-D stereo pair and can be viewed in dimension through the "free vision" process of slightly crossing your eyes.

5
Design Firm: Shapiro Design Associates Inc.
Art Director: Ellen Shapiro
Designer: Terri Bogaards
Illustrator: Terri Bogaards
Client: Institute for Mental Health Initiatives
Purpose or Occasion: Public Service Campaign
Number of Colors: 2

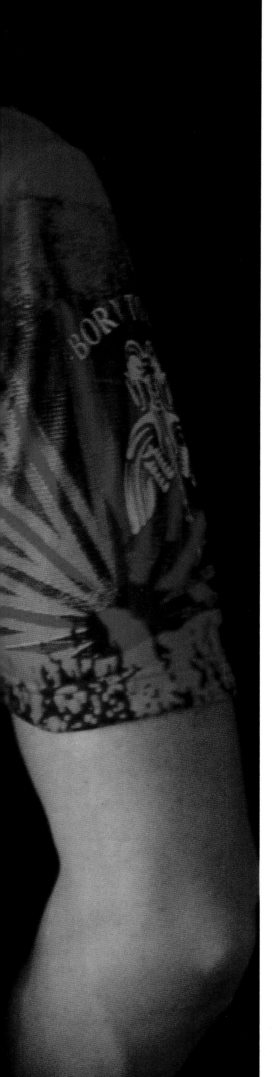

1
Design Firm: Hornall Anderson Design Works, Inc.
Art Director: Jack Anderson
Designer: Jack Anderson/Brian O'Neill
Client: Gang of Seven
Purpose or Occasion: Bicycle racing team
Number of Colors: 2

2
Design Firm: THARP DID IT
Art Director: Rick Tharp
Designer: Rick Tharp
Client: Sebastiani Vineyards
Purpose or Occasion: Celebrates the Fall release
of this Nouveau Wine.
Number of Colors: 5

1

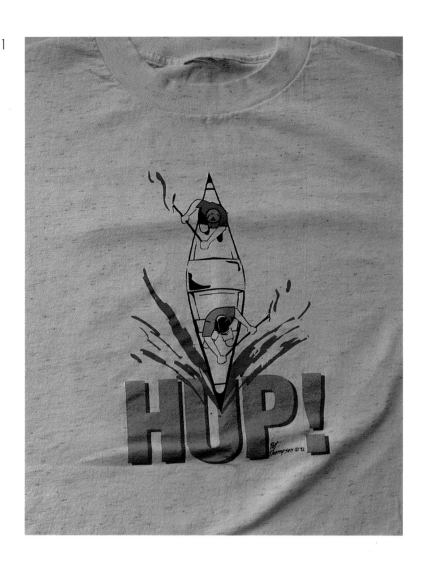

2

1
Design Firm: Real Impressions
Art Director: Patrick Thompson
Designer: Patrick Thompson
Illustrator: Patrick Thompson
Client: Ausable Canoe Marathon
Purpose or Occasion: Annual event in Grayling, Mich.
Number of Colors: 2

2
Design Firm: Karyl Klopp Design
Art Director: Karyl Klopp
Designer: Karyl Klopp
Illustrator: Karyl Klopp
Client: Cityside Restaurant
Purpose or Occasion: Summer
Number of Colors: 6

3
Design Firm: Glazer Gaphics
Art Director: Nancy Glazer
Designer: Nancy Glazer
Client: Pecos River Learning Centers
Purpose or Occasion: Retail
Number of Colors: 5

The images represent each outdoor adventure event; "the pole," "the zip line," and "the wall."

4
Design Firm: Sibley/Peteet Design
Art Director: David Beck
Designer: David Beck
Illustrator: David Beck
Client: National Kidney Foundation
Purpose or Occasion: Turtle Creek Run
Number of Colors: 5

4

1
Design Firm: Masterpiece Teez
Art Director: Christina Solomon
Designer: CDS Corporation
Illustrator: Pablo Picasso original artwork "Lady In a Chair"
Purpose or Occasion: Retail

2
Design Firm: Masterpiece Teez
Art Director: Christina Solomon
Designer: CDS Corporation
Illustrator: Pablo Picasso original artwork "Studio
with Plasterhead"
Purpose or Occasion: Retail
Number of Colors: 7

2

1

2

3

1
Design Firm: Punch Design Inc.
Art Director: Rick Korab
Designer: Rick Rorab
Illustrator: Rick Korab
Client: One Man Merchandising
Purpose or Occasion: Retail
Number of Colors: 6

2
Illustrator: Joan C. Hollingsworth
Purpose or Occasion: Self Promotion

3
Design Firm: Jim Lange Design
Art Director: Jim Lange
Designer: Jim Lange
Illustrator: Jim Lange
Client: Chicago Sun-Times
Purpose or Occasion: Official shirts for world's
largest triathlon
Number of Colors: 3

4
Design Firm: Raymond Bennett Design
Art Director: Raymond Bennett
Designer: Victoria McNeill
Client: NSW Model Yacht Association
Purpose or Occasion: National Championships
Number of Colors: 1

5
Design Firm: KaiserDicken
Art Director: Craig Dicken/ Debra Kaiser
Designer: Debra Kaiser
Illustrator: Debra Kaiser
Client: Sailworks
Purpose or Occasion: Summer's End Regatta
Number of Colors: 3

1

Aqui me pinté yo, Frida Kahlo, con
la imagen del espejo. Tengo 3 kum
y es el mes de Julio de mil nove

1
Design Firm: Masterpiece Teez
Art Director: Christina Solomon
Designer: CDS Corporation
Illustrator: Frida Kahlo original artwork "Unbound Hair"
Purpose or Occasion: Retail

2
Design Firm: Masterpiece Teez
Art Director: Christina Solomon
Designer: CDS Corporation
Illustrator: Frida Kahlo original artwork "Bound Hair"
Purpose or Occasion: Retail

1
Design Firm: Creative Arts Group
Art Director: Gaylord Bennitt
Designer: Gaylord Bennitt
Illustrator: Gaylord Bennitt
Client: International Canoe Federation
World Championships
Purpose or Occasion: Retail
Number of Colors: 6

2
Design Firm: Bright & Associates
Art Director: Konrad Bright
Designer: Konrad Bright
Client: Ketchum Advertising
Purpose or Occasion: Logo
Number of Colors: 4

3
Design Firm: Bright & Associates
Art Director: Konrad Bright
Designer: Konrad Bright
Illustrator: Konrad Bright
Client: Terranova Construction
Purpose or Occasion: Logo for company
Number of Colors: 3

3

3

1
Design Firm: Masterpiece Teez
Art Director: Christina Solomon
Designer: CDS Corporation
Illustrator: Marc Chagall original artwork "I & The Village"
Purpose or Occasion: Retail
Number of Colors: 4

2
Design Firm: Creative Arts Group
Art Director: Gaylord Bennitt
Designer: Gaylord Bennitt
Illustrator: Gaylord Bennitt
Client: Reno Rugby Club Tournament
Purpose or Occasion: Promotional
Number of Colors: 3

3
Design Firm: B.E.P. Design Group
Art Director: Jean J. Evrard
Client: Harry De Vlaminck
Purpose or Occasion: Snowcat Rally in Canada
Number of Colors: 2

4
Design Firm: Aardvark Studio
Illustrator: Andy Lackow
Client: Mega Designs
Purpose or Occasion: Retail

4

MARINA DEL REY OUTRIGGER CANOE CLUB

Design Firm: Bright & Associates
Art Director: Konrad Bright
Designer: Konrad Bright
Illustrator: Konrad Bright
Client: Marina Del Rey Outrigger Canoe Club
Purpose or Occasion: 1992 Moliki Outrigger Canoe Race
Number of Colors: 1

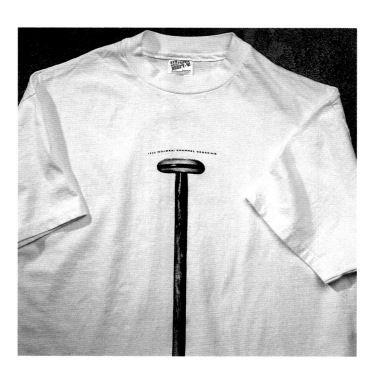

BUILDING
BLOCKS

Success

CENTRAL RUSH TEAM

NORTHWE
UNIVERS

WINTER RUSH 1992

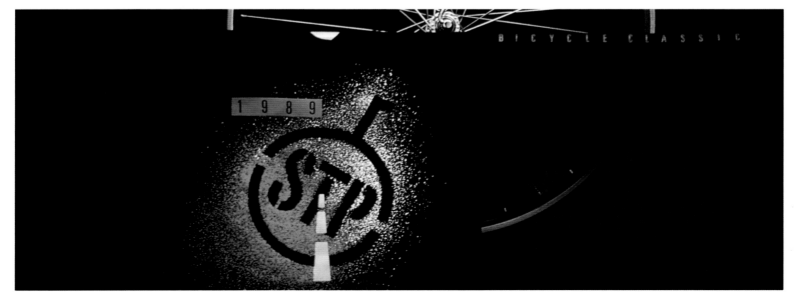

BICYCLE CLASSIC

1989
STP

1

3

1
Design Firm: Sayles Graphic Design
Art Director: John Sayles
Designer: John Sayles
Illustrator: John Sayles
Client: Northwestern University
Purpose or Occasion: Promotional
Number of Colors: 2

2
Design Firm: Hornall Anderson Design Works, Inc.
Art Director: Jack Anderson
Designer: Jack Anderson/Jani Drewfs/David Bates
Illustrator: David Bates
Client: Cascade Bicycle Club
Purpose or Occasion: Bicycle event
Number of Colors: 5

Promotes the nation's largest 200-mile bicycle event.

3
Design Firm: Sibley/Peteet Design
Art Director: Rex Peteet
Designer: Rex Peteet
Illustrator: Rex Peteet
Client: Fuzztones Band
Purpose or Occasion: Promotional
Number of Colors: 5

4
Design Firm: Hornall Anderson Design Works, Inc.
Art Director: Jack Anderson
Designer: Jack Anderson/Denise Weir/
Jani Drewfs/Julie Tanagi-Lock
Illustrator: Jani Drewfs/Jack Anderson
Client: K2 Corporation
Number of Colors: 4

4

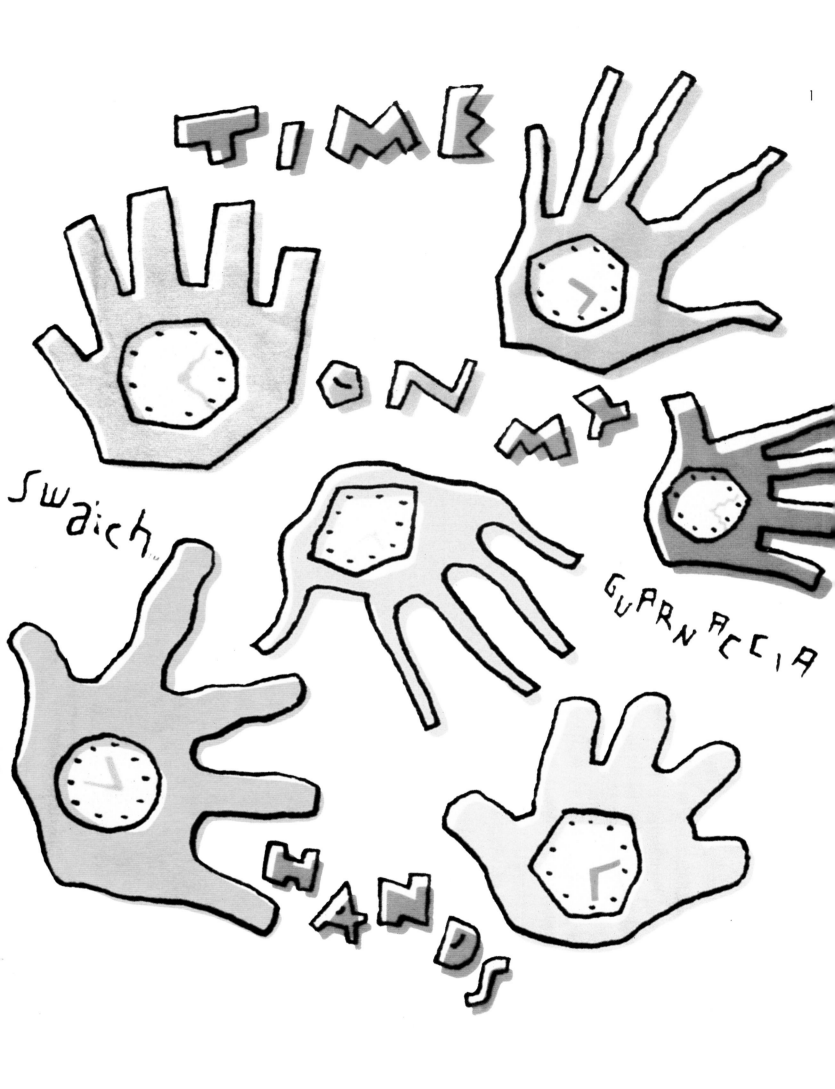

2

1
Art Director: Cheryl Chung
Designer: Steven Guarnaccia
Illustrator: Steven Guarnaccia
Client: Swatch
Purpose or Occasion: Promotional
Number of Colors: 7

2
Design Firm: Sayles Graphic Design
Art Director: John Sayles
Designer: John Sayles
Illustrator: John Sayles
Client: Open Bible Churches
Purpose or Occasion: Event Memorabilia
Number of Colors: 3

3
Design Firm: Sommese Design
Art Director: Lanny Sommese
Designer: Lanny Sommese
Illustrator: Lanny Sommese
Client: Central Pennsylvania Festival of the Arts
Purpose or Occasion: 25th Anniversary Festival
of the Visual and Performing Arts
Number of Colors: 2

3

1

2

1-2
Design Firm: Sayles Graphic Design
Art Director: John Sayles
Designer: John Sayles
Illustrator: John Sayles
Client: Wienie Wagon
Purpose or Occasion: Promotional
Number of Colors: 2

3
Design Firm: Charles S. Anderson Design Co.
Art Director: Charles S. Anderson / Daniel Olson
Designer: Daniel Olson / Charles S. Anderson
Illustrator: Charles S. Anderson / Randall Dahlk
Client: Hollywood Paramount Products
Purpose or Occasion: Retail
Number of Colors: 1

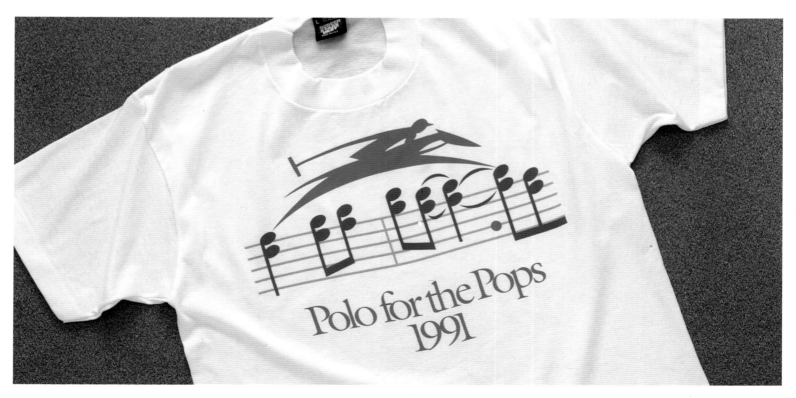

1
Design Firm: Sibley/Peteet Design
Art Director: Rex Peteet
Designer: Rex Peteet
Illustrator: Rex Peteet
Client: GSD&M
Purpose or Occasion: New corporate identity
Number of Colors: 5

2
Design Firm: Conge Design
Art Director: Sue Kemp
Designer: Bob Conge
Illustrator: Bob Conge
Client: Screen Machine U.S.A.
Purpose or Occasion: Retail
Number of Colors: 4
Printer: Screen Machine USA, Rochester, NY

3
Design Firm: Dally Advertising
Art Director: Randy Padorr-Black
Designer: Randy Padorr-Black
Illustrator: Randy Padorr-Black
Client: Fort Worth Symphony
Purpose or Occasion: Fundraiser
Number of Colors: 3
Printer: Lonestar Sportswear, Ft. Worth, TX

4
Design Firm: Mervil Paylor Design
Art Director: Mervil M. Paylor
Designer: Mervil M. Paylor
Illustrator: Mervil M. Paylor
Client: Ron Chapple Photography
Purpose or Occasion: Promotional
Number of Colors: 4

4

1

2

3

1
Design Firm: Marlene Montgomery Design
Art Director: Marlene Montgomery
Designer: Marlene Montgomery
Illustrator: Marlene Montgomery
Client: Marlene Montgomery Design
Purpose or Occasion: Retail

Wrap-around and front and back designs.

2
Design Firm: Marlene Montgomery Design
Art Director: Marlene Montgomery
Designer: Marlene Montgomery
Illustrator: Marlene Montgomery
Client: Marlene Montgomery Design
Purpose or Occasion: Retail
Number of Colors: 2

Wrap-around and front and back designs.

3
Design Firm: The Bennitt Group
Art Director: Dave Dittman
Designer: Gaylord Bennitt
Illustrator: Gaylord Bennitt
Client: Eco-Safe Textiles
Purpose or Occasion: P.A.W.S. Fundraiser
Number of Colors: 4

Water base ink - no solvents bio-degradeable shirt.

4
Design Firm: Hornall Anderson Design Works
Art Director: Jack Anderson
Designer: Jack Anderson/Julia LaPine/ Lian Ng
Illustrator: Julia LaPine/ Brian O'Neill
Client: Washington Software Association
Purpose or Occasion: Fourth Annual WSA Halloween Ball
Number of Colors: 2

THE RIORDON DESIGN GROUP INC.

1992 MOLOKAI RACING TEAM

MARINA
DEL   REY

OUTRIGGER CANOE CLUB

3

1
Design Firm: Riordon Design Group Inc.
Art Director: Ric Riordon
Designer: Ric Riordon
Illustrator: Dan Wheaton
Client: The Riordon Design Group Inc.
Purpose or Occasion: Self Promotion
Number of Colors: 9

Computer-generated illustration.

2
Design Firm: Bright & Associates
Art Director: Konrad Bright
Designer: Konrad Bright
Illustrator: Konrad Bright
Client: Marina Del Rey Outrigger Canoe Team
Purpose or Occasion: Team shirts
Number of Colors: 4

3
Design Firm: Sommese Design
Art Director: Kristin Sommese/Lanny Sommese
Designer: Kristin Sommese/Lanny Sommese
Client: Happy Valley Brew
Purpose or Occasion: Promotional
Number of Colors: 4

1

2

3

1
Design Firm: Dally Advertising
Art Director: Randy Padorr-Black
Designer: Randy Padorr-Black
Illustrator: Randy Padorr-Black
Client: Downtown Dallas YMCA
Purpose or Occasion: 10K Run/ Thanksgiving Day
Number of Colors: 6
Printer: Silverwing Productions, Dallas, TX

2
Design Firm: Real Impressions
Art Director: Patrick Thompson
Designer: Patrick Thompson
Illustrator: Patrick Thompson
Client: Ausable Canoe Marathon
Purpose or Occasion: Annual pledge relay committee
Number of Colors: 3

3
Design Firm: Studio MD
Art Director: Glenn Mitsui/Jesse Doguilo/ Randy Lim
Illustrator: Glenn Mitsui
Client: Letraset
Purpose or Occasion: Conference T-shirt
Number of Colors: 1 and 2

4
Design Firm: Sommese Design
Art Director: Kristin Sommese
Designer: Kristin Sommese
Illustrator: Kristin Sommese
Client: Penn State Beta Sigma Beta Fraternity
Purpose or Occasion: Annual charity boat race
Number of Colors: 4

5
Design Firm: John Evans Design
Art Director: John Evans
Designer: John Evans
Illustrator: John Evans
Client: Sweatyme
Purpose or Occasion: Promotional
Number of Colors: 4

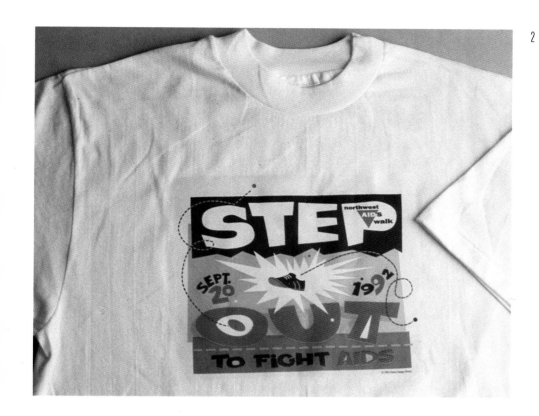

1
Design Firm: Zedwear
Art Director: George Mimnaugh/John Klaja
Designer: George Mimnaugh/John Klaja
Illustrator: Randy Lyhus
Client: Zedwear
Purpose or Occasion: Retail
Number of Colors: 4
Title: "Spots"

2
Design Firm: Gable Design Group
Art Director: Tony Gable/Jana Nishi
Designer: Karin Yamagiwa
Illustrator: Karin Yamagiwa
Client: N.W. AIDS Foundation
Purpose or Occasion: 1992 Walk-A-Thon
Number of Colors: 4

1

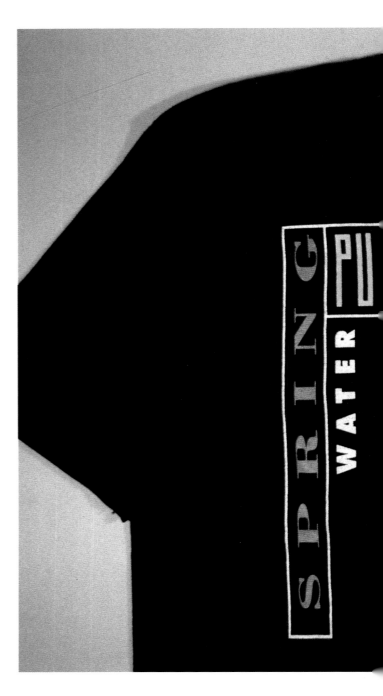

1
Design Firm: Bright & Associates
Art Director: Konrad Bright
Designer: Konrad Bright
Illustrator: Konrad Bright
Client: Lopez Electric
Purpose or Occasion: Logo
Number of Colors: 4 on back, 2 on front

2
Design Firm: Sommese Design
Art Director: Kristin Sommese/ Lanny Sommese
Designer: Kristin Sommese
Illustrator: Lanny Sommese
Client: Aquapenn Spring Water Co.
Purpose or Occasion: Pomotional
Number of Colors: 4

3
Design Firm: Aardvark Studio
Illustrator: Andy Lackow
Client: Mega Designs
Purpose or Occasion: Retail

B.F. Day Scho

© 1990 Design & Illustr

1
Design Firm: Gable Design Group
Art Director: Tony Gable
Designer: Kris Matsuyama/Tony Gable
Illustrator: Kris Matsuyama
Client: B.F. Day Elementary School
Purpose or Occasion: New logo
Number of Colors: 3

2
Design Firm: Creative Services
Designer: Ron J. Pride
Illustrator: Ron J. Pride
Client: Narcotics Education Inc.
Purpose or Occasion: Promotional
Number of Colors: 3

2

ol

Design Group

1

FASHION ISLAND
NEWPORT BEACH CALIFORNIA

2

3

4

5

Florida

1
Design Firm: Sibley/Peteet Design
Art Director: Don Sibley
Designer: Don Sibley
Illustrator: Don Sibley
Client: Fashion Island Shopping Center
Number of Colors: 7

2
Design Firm: Cyrk
Art Director: Dave Saltonstall
Designer: Dave Saltonstall
Client: Cyrk Retail
Number of Colors: 8

3
Design Firm: Cyrk, Inc.
Art Director: Robert D. Killam
Designer: Bob Killam
Illustrator: Bob Killam
Client: J.C. Penney/ Cyrk Shirts
Purpose or Occasion: Retail
Number of Colors: 6

4
Design Firm: DeRossett Design
Designer: Michael DeRossett
Illustrator: Michael DeRossett
Client: Progressive Beauty Enterprises
Purpose or Occasion: Limited edition sweatshirts
Number of Colors: 1

All Aveda products are derived from natural herbs
and plants.

5
Design Firm: CTM Manufacturing, Inc.
Art Director: Robert H. Mayworth
Designer: Robert H. Mayworth
Illustrator: Robert H. Mayworth
Client: CTM's "Coastal Wear"
Purpose or Occasion: Retail
Number of Colors: 4 with 5th color glitter

"Waterlilies" was laser separated with embellishments
done by hand.

1

2

1, 3
Design Firm: John Evans Design
Art Director: John Evans
Designer: John Evans
Illustrator: John Evans
Client: Exchange Athletic Club
Purpose or Occasion: Retail
Number of Colors: 4

2
Design Firm: Jim Lange Design
Art Director: Jim Lange
Designer: Jim Lange
Illustrator: Jim Lange
Client: Downtown Sports Club
Purpose or Occasion: Squash Tournament Finals
Number of Colors: 4

DALLAS WHITE ROCK MARATHON

1
Design Firm: Sibley/Peteet Design
Art Director: John Evans
Designer: John Evans
Illustrator: John Evans
Client: White Rock Marathon
Purpose or Occasion: Promotional
Number of Colors: 6

2
Design Firm: Marc English: Design
Designer: Marc English
Client: Buffalo Boys
Purpose or Occasion: Buffalo Boys Club Shirt
Number of Colors: 2

3
Design Firm: Real Impressions
Art Director: Patrick Thompson
Designer: Patrick Thompson
Illustrator: Patrick Thompson
Client: Ausable Canoe Marathon
Purpose or Occasion: Promotional
Number of Colors: 4

New York

New York

New York

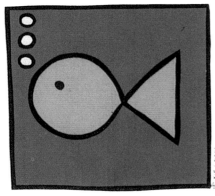

Fish

Dinner

Octopus

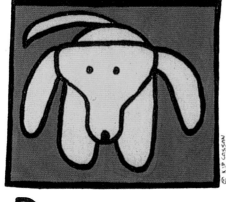

Dog

Cat

Football

Chaos

Dinosaur

Cow

Pig

Heart

Moon&Stars

Design Firm: Kip Kids of New York
Art Director: Kipton P. Cosson
Designer: Kipton P. Cosson
Illustrator: Kipton P. Cosson
Purpose or Occasion: Retail

directory

Aardvark Studio
Andy Lackow
7004 Boulevard East #29-C
Guttenberg, NJ 07093

Amber Productions, Inc.
John Garrison
414 West 4th Avenue
Columbus, OH 43201

Art Guy Studios
James F. Kraus
195 West Canton Street
Boston, MA 02116

BEP Design Group
Jean-Jaques Evrard
Rue des Mimosas 44
B-1030 Brussels
BELGIUM

Bright & Associates
Keith Bright
901 Abbot Kinney Blvd.
Venice, CA 90291

CAS The Sign Systems
Company
David Rothstein
10909 Tuxford Street
Sun Valley, CA 99352

CTM Manufacturing
Pam Bravo
4773 58th Avenue N.
St. Petersburg, FL 33714

Carmichael Lynch
Peter Wecke
800 Hennepin Avenue
Minneapolis, MN 55403

Charles S. Anderson Design Co.
Rice Davis
30 N. First Street
Minneapolis, MN 55401

Conge Design
Robin Banker
28 Harper Street
Rochester, NY 14607

Creative Arts Group
Gaylord Bennitt
961 Venture Court
Sacramento, CA 95825

Creative Services
55 W. Oak Ridge Dr.
Hagerstown, MD 21740

Cyrk
Tom Gardner
3 Pond Road
Gloucester, MA 01930

Dally Advertising
Randy Padorr-Black
1320 South University
Suite 501
Fort Worth, TX 76107

DeRossett Design
Michael DeRossett
10221 West 81st Terrace
#153, Overland Park, KS
66204-5708

Dogfish Design
Korey Peterson
P.O. Box 2754

Gig Harbor, WA 98335
Ed the Dog Productions
P.O. Box 8727
Wichita, KS 67208

Electric Design
Joette Spinelli
200 East 26th Street
New York, NY 10010

Epstein Gutzwiller Schultz
& Partners
Marla Gutzwiller
11427 Bellflower Road
Cleveland, OH 44106

Gable Design Group
Tony Gable
1809 7th Avenue #310
Seattle, WA 98101

Gardner Design
100 North 6th St. #901-A
Minneapolis, MN 55403

Glazer Graphics
Nancy Glazer
Route 14, Box 738C
Santa Fe, NM 87505

Gunnar Swanson Design
Office
Gunnar Swanson
739 Indiana Avenue
Venice, CA 90291-2728

Joan C. Hollingsworth
2824 NE 22
Portland, OR 97212

Hornall Anderson Design
Works
Jack Anderson
1008 Western Avenue
Floor 6, Seattle, WA 98104

Jim Lange Design
Jim Lange
203 N. Wabash Avenue
#1312
Chicago, IL 60601-2414

John Evans Design
John Evans
3932 Hatherly Drive
Plano, TX 75023

The Graphic Design Office of
Jim Vandergrift
4575 A. Amerald Street
Capitola, CA 95010

Judi Radice Design
Consultant
Judi Radice
950 Battery Street
3rd Floor
San Francisco, CA 94111

Kaiserdicken
Craig Dicken
149 Cherry Street
Burlington, VT 05401

Karyl Klopp Design
Karyl Klopp
5209 8th Avenue
Charlestown, MA 02129

Kip Kids of New York
Kipton P. Cosson
85 Christopher St #5B
New York, NY 10014

Lance Anderson Design
Lance Anderson
22 Margrave Place
San Francisco, CA 94133

Leslie Evans Design &
Illustration
Leslie Evans
17 Bay Street
Watertown, MA 02172

Letvin Design
Carolyn Letvin
96 Elm Street
Upton, MA 01568

Line 3 Design
Eric Behrenfeld
1440 N. Dayton
Chicago, IL 60622

Marc English: Design
Marc English
37 Wellington Avenue
Lexington, MA 02173-7110

Masterpiece Teez
136 S. Roxbury #5
Beverly Hills, CA 90212

Manigault Design
Richard K. Manigault
679 Vanderbilt Avenue
Brooklyn, NY 11238

Marlene Montgomery Design
5720 W. Huron
Chicago, IL 60644

Melinda Beck
444th Place Apt. 2
Brooklyn, NY 11231

Mervil Paylor Design
Mervil Paylor
1917 Lennox Avenue
Charlotte, NC 28203

Michael Carr Design
Michael Timble
1243 W. Belmont
Chicago, IL 60657

Michael Stanard Inc.
Marcos Chavez
1000 Main Street
Evanston, IL 60202

Micrografx Creative Services
Group
Karen Jacobi Smith
1303 Arapaho Road
Richardson, TX 75081

Mike Quon Design Office
Mike Quon
568 Broadway
New York, NY 10012

Mike Salisbury
Communications
2200 Amapola Court
Torrance, CA 90501

Mirror Image Inc./Fotofolio
Colin Cheer
251 Albany Street
Cambridge, MA 02139

Morla Design
Jennifer Morla
463 Bryant Street
San Francisco, CA 94107

Musikar Design
Sharon Musikar
7524 Indian Hills Drive
Rockville, MD 20855

Nessim & Assoc./Misako
Barbara Nessim
63 Green Street
New York City, NY 10012

Paper Shrine Inc.
Paul Dean
604 France Street
Baton Rouge, LA 70802

Pear Graphics
Kim Farnham
2224 Pierce Creek Road
Binghamton, NY 13903

Pictogram Studio
Stephanie Hooton
1740 U Street NW, Suite #2
Washington, DC 20009

Propaganda
Mike Timble
1243 W. Belmont Avenue
Chicago, IL 60657

Punch Design
Rick Korab
475 Cleveland Ave North
#222, St. Louis, MN
55104-5051

The Pushpin Group
Ellen Serluco
215 Park Avenue So.
New York, NY 10003

Raymond Bennett Design
Assoc. Ltd.
Raymond Bennett
3/345 Pacific Hwy
Crows Nest NSW
AUSTRALIA

Reactor Art & Design
51 Camden Street
Toronto, ON M5V 1V2
CANADA

Real Impressions
Pat Thompson
2850 Kennely Road
Saginaw, MI 48609

Richard C. Fish Associates
1733 Academy Lane
Havertown, PA 19083

Riordon Design Group, Inc.
Ric Riordon
1001 Queen Street West
Mississauga, Ontario
L5H 4E1 CANADA

Sabin Design
Tracy Sabin
13476 Ridley Road
San Diego, CA 92129

Sayles Graphic Design
John Sayles
308 Eighth Street
Des Moines, IA 50309

Segura Inc.
Carlos Segura
540 North Lake Shore Dr.
Suite 324
Chicago, IL 60611-3431

Sergio Illustration
512 S.W. Broadway, Suite 225
Portland, OR 97205

Shapiro Design Associates, Inc.
Ellen Shapiro
141 Fifth Avenue
New York, NY 10010

Sibley/Peteet Design, Inc.
Rex Peteet
965 Slocum
Dallas, TX 77207

Sommese Design
Lanny Sommese
481 Glenn Road
State College, PA 16803

Stefan Georg Originals
2442 Cerrillos Rd #28
Santa Fe, NM 87501

Steven Guarnaccia
430 W. 14th Street
New York, NY 10014

Studio MD
Cindy Chin
1512 Alaskan Way
Seattle, WA 98101-1514

Ted Hansen Design Associates
Ted Hansen
1955 Fourth Avenue
San Diego, CA 92101

Temel West Inc.
Chris Blakeman
819 1/2 West Hays
Boise, ID 83702

Tharp Did It
Rick Tharp
50 University Avenue
Suite 21
Los Gatos, CA 95030

The Bennett Group
Gaylord Bennett
961 Venture Court
Sacramento, CA 95825

The Lee Communications
Network
Lovelace Lee
1950 1/2 La Salle Avenue
Los Angeles, CA 90018

Tilka Design
Jane Tilka
1400 West Lake Street
#314
Minneapolis, MN 55408

Vaughn/Wedeen Creative
Rick Vaughn
407 Rio Grande NW
Albuquerque, NM 87104

Visual Dialogue
Fritz Klaetke
429 Columbus Avenue #1
Boston, MA 02116

WGBH
Christopher Pullman
125 Western Avenue
Boston, MA 02134

Zedwear
John Klaja
1718 Main Street NW
#101
Washington, DC 20036

index